D0296548

30131 04727924 2

LONDON BOROUGH OF BARNET

Author:

Ian Graham studied applied physics at the City University, London. He then took a postgraduate degree in journalism, specialising in science and technology. Since becoming a freelance author and journalist, he has written more than one hundred children's non-fiction books.

Artist:

David Antram was born in Brighton, England, in 1958. He studied at Eastbourne College of Art and then worked in advertising for fifteen years before becoming a full-time artist. He has illustrated many children's non-fiction books.

Series creator:

David Salariya was born in Dundee, Scotland. He has illustrated a wide range of books and has created and designed many new series for publishers in the UK and overseas. He established The Salariya Book Company in 1989. He lives in Brighton with his wife, illustrator Shirley Willis, and their son Jonathan.

Editor: **Stephen Haynes**

Editorial Assistants:

Mark Williams, Tanya Kant

Published in Great Britain in 2008 by
Book House, an imprint of
The Salariya Book Company Ltd
25 Marlborough Place, Brighton BN1 1UB
www.salariya.com
www.book-house.co.uk

HB ISBN-13: 978-1-906370-21-3
PB ISBN-13: 978-1-906370-22-0

SALARIYA

1 3 5 7 9 8 6 4 2

A CIP catalogue record for this book is available
from the British Library.

Printed and bound in China.
Printed on paper from sustainable sources.

Avoid being in the First Submarine!

Written by
Ian Graham

Illustrated by
David Antram

Created and designed by
David Salariya

The Danger Zone

BOOK HOUSE

Contents

Introduction

t's 1863. You are an engineer working in a machine shop in Alabama. You build and repair boilers, steam engines and pipework of all kinds.

You can turn your hand to any sort of metalwork, but today you are starting work on one of the strangest jobs you've ever done. You're cutting up a water boiler to make a submarine! It's to be called the *H. L. Hunley* after Horace Hunley, one of the men who put up the money to pay for it. Time is short and you'll have to work fast. The American Civil War is raging between the Confederate States in the south and the rest of the United States (the Union). The Confederacy needs the submarine to attack Union warships blockading the South. You can hardly believe that men are actually going to dive under the water in it. You're glad you're only building the thing. You really wouldn't want to serve in an early submarine!

Just wait till you see this amazing new invention!

▨ *Union states*

▨ *Confederate states*

▨ *Border states*

▨ *Western territories*

CANADA

MEXICO

Alabama

The first submarines

The *Hunley* isn't the first submarine ever, but you're hoping it will be the first really successful one. Drawings and designs for submarines were made in the 16th century. In 1578 an Englishman, William Bourne, designed an underwater rowing boat, but he didn't build it. The first real submarine was built in the 1620s by the Dutch inventor Cornelis Drebbel. It was tested in the River Thames in London. The first American submarine was an egg-shaped craft called the *Turtle*, built in 1775 by David Bushnell. By the 1860s, engineers like you are making submarines out of metal.

THE ITALIAN artist and engineer Leonardo da Vinci made a drawing of a submarine in 1513, but he didn't actually build it.

Screw

Torpedo

Propeller

Rudder

THE SUBMARINE

Cornelis Drebbel built in the 1620s may have looked like this (left). It was a wooden rowing boat, covered with leather to keep the water out. Twelve oarsmen rowed it. One of its dives is said to have lasted three hours.

THE *NAUTILUS* (below)

was built by an American engineer, Robert Fulton, in 1800. It was covered with copper. When it was on the surface, the crew raised a sail. Underwater, they turned a propeller.

What manner of thing is this, mother?

'Tis a new one on me, child.

Squawk!

THE *TURTLE* submarine (left) was built for war. It was meant to be steered up against a ship, then a bomb (called a torpedo) would be screwed into the ship's hull. The *Turtle* would slip away and then the torpedo would explode. But it didn't work.

Cracking the problems

Engineers like you have been trying for centuries to solve the problems of building submarines. They had to figure out how to make a boat dive underwater. More importantly, they had to work out how to bring it up to the surface again! And how can a submarine be powered? You could try to find a way of using a steam engine, but it's simpler to get the crew to turn a propeller by hand. When you try this in your workshop, it's easy – you can spin the propeller really fast. But it's much harder to turn it in water, because water is so much denser than air.

AIR. The first submarines have no air tanks. The crew can only breathe the air that was in the submarine before it dived. They have to surface before it runs out!

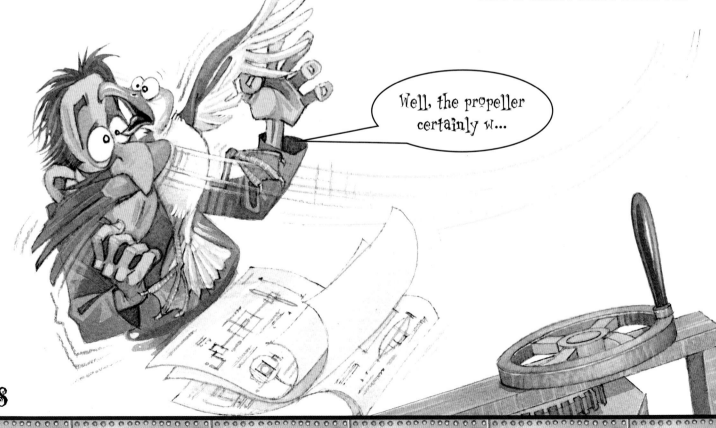

Well, the propeller certainly w...

Handy hint

Remember to go to the toilet before you dive!

LIGHT. It's dark inside an early submarine. Candles provide a dim, flickering light – just enough for the crew to work by.

DIVING. In order to dive, a submarine needs to become heavier. A valve lets seawater flow into tanks inside the boat, called ballast tanks.

SURFACING. To bring the submarine up again, water has to be forced out of the ballast tanks. It is pumped out by hand – more hard work!

Civil War submarines

Both sides in the Civil War build submarines to attack each other's warships. The first of them, the US Navy's *Alligator* and the Confederate submarine *Pioneer*, are launched in 1862. Neither of them is a great success. While *Alligator* is being towed by another ship, it has to be cut free during a storm, and sinks. *Pioneer* is lost to Union forces when they overrun its home port of New Orleans. The engineers learn from their experience and go on to build better submarines.

Underwater arms race

PIONEER is nearly 10 metres long and made of iron. It's operated by a crew of three – the captain and two men to turn its propeller.

THE CONFEDERATE NAVY'S *David* steam torpedo boats look like submarines, but they can't go completely under the water.

Handy hint

Wrap up warm, because there's no heating in an early submarine!

THE SECOND Union submarine is the *Intelligent Whale* (below). Construction begins in 1863, but it's still not finished when the war ends.

THE FIRST Union submarine is the *Alligator* (above). It is about 15 metres long. At first it has oars. Later, a propeller replaces them.

AMERICAN DIVER (right), built in 1863, is the second Confederate submarine. Attempts to power it with an electric motor fail, because the motor isn't powerful enough. Steam power fails too, so it is powered by hand.

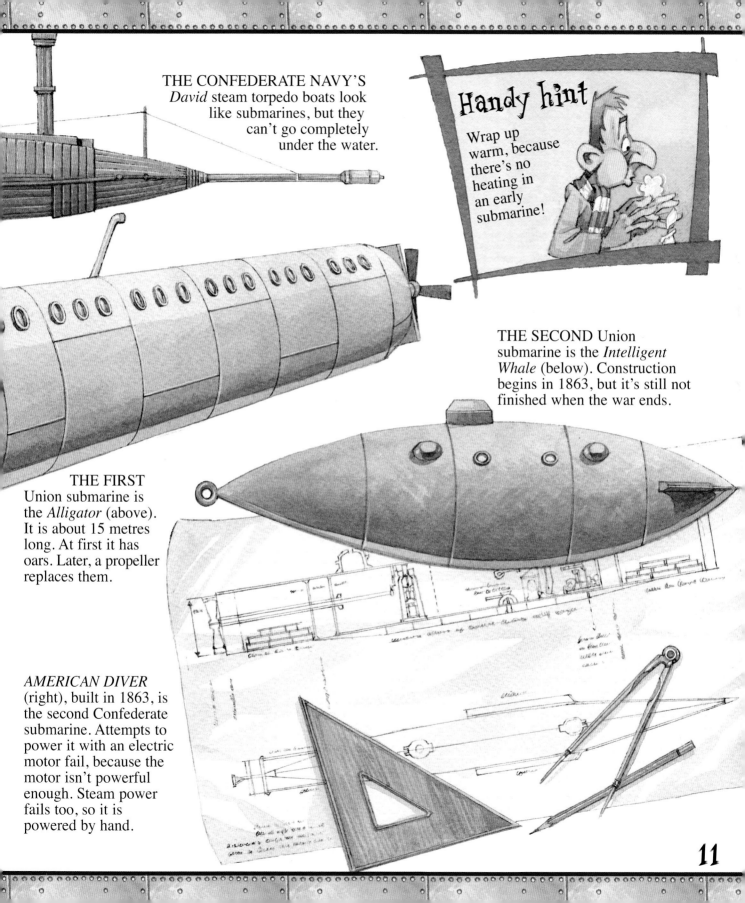

Mr Hunley's submarine

The first stage in building the *H. L. Hunley* is to find a boiler from a steamboat that's about the right size. The one you pick is an iron cylinder about 7.6 metres long and 1.2 metres across. You cut it in two along its length and insert two flat iron strips 30 cm wide. Then you add a tapering nose and tail. These will help the submarine to slice through the water more easily. Heavy iron plates bolted to the bottom add extra weight to help it sink.

Cutwater: this helps to streamline the entrance/exit hatch.

Forward hatch

Bow (front end)

Pole or spar for a torpedo (see page 22) is attached here.

Fin, or dive plane: tilting this down or up helps to make the Hunley dive and surface again.

Ballast tanks at each end can be filled with water to make the submarine heavier.

Rudder: swivels from side to side to steer the submarine.

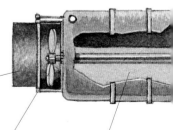

Propeller

Aft ballast tank

On a boat, forward *means 'front'* and aft *means 'rear'. If you want to sound like a sailor, say 'forrad' rather than 'for-ward'.*

Handy hint

Don't eat too much – you might not fit through those narrow hatches.

Snorkel tubes can be raised to let fresh air in – but only when the submarine is very close to the surface.

Deadlights: these small, round glass windows let in light when the boat is on the surface.

Aft hatch

Stern (back end)

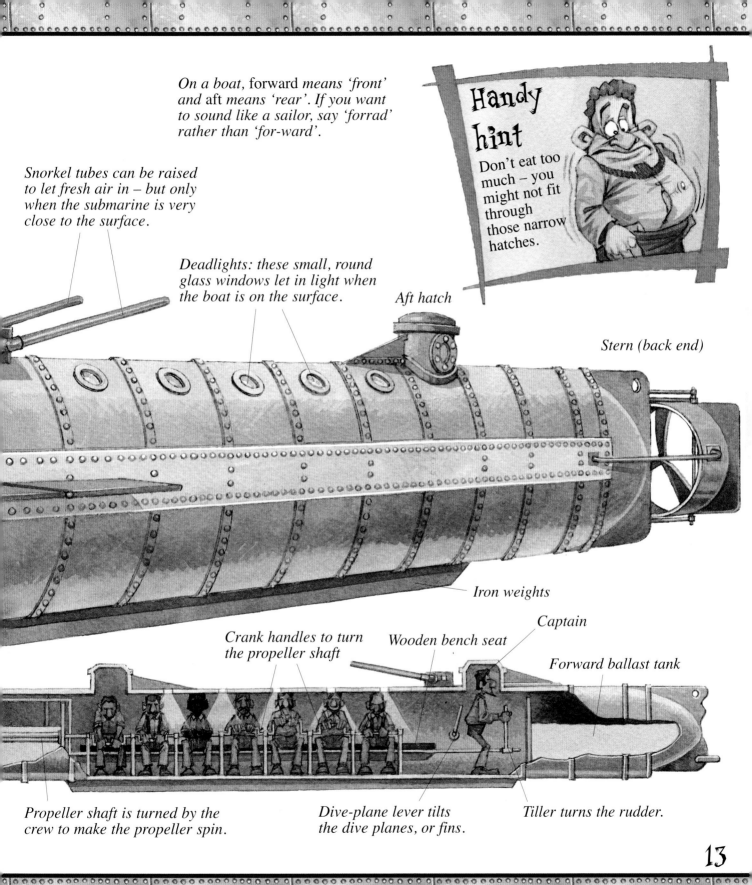

Iron weights

Crank handles to turn the propeller shaft

Wooden bench seat

Captain

Forward ballast tank

Propeller shaft is turned by the crew to make the propeller spin.

Dive-plane lever tilts the dive planes, or fins.

Tiller turns the rudder.

Inside the Hunley

Imagine what the *Hunley*'s crew must think of their new craft the first time they see it. Most of them are used to serving on wooden sailing ships. Their new vessel doesn't look much like a warship, or any sort of ship at all! It's a small metal tube that looks as though it's barely able to stay afloat. There are no masts or sails, no decks and no guns. When the sailors look down into the open hatches, it's pitch-black inside. But now it's time to get on board and practise going to war. One by one, the sailors climb down into the darkness.

Breathe in!

IT'S A SQUEEZE to get into the submarine. The hatches are only 35 cm wide. When you do get inside, there isn't much room. From floor to ceiling, it's about 1.2 metres high. Even a child couldn't stand up straight in here!

Maybe I should go on a diet...

And to think I volunteered for this!

TAKE GREAT CARE not to bang your head on anything.

ONLY THE CAPTAIN can see outside through small glass ports. He steers with the tiller and dives by using the dive-plane lever.

Diving and surfacing

TILTING the fins down makes the sub dive deeper. Water pushing against the fins forces its nose down.

The whole crew has to work together to make the *Hunley* dive safely. While the others turn the propeller to move the submarine forwards, the captain opens a valve called a seacock. This lets seawater flood into the ballast tank in the submarine's nose. The weight of the water makes the nose heavier and the boat starts to sink. At the same time, a sailor near the stern (back end) of the submarine opens another seacock. This lets water rush into the ballast tank at the stern. Having a ballast tank at each end keeps the submarine level as it dives. To go even deeper, the captain pushes a lever to tilt the fins, or dive planes.

A DEPTH GAUGE on the wall shows the captain how far below the water's surface the submarine is. It needs to go deep enough to pass under an enemy ship, without hitting the seabed.

THE CAPTAIN steers by moving a lever (the tiller) from side to side to swivel the rudder at the stern.

Snorkel tube

TO SURFACE, the fins are tilted up and water is pumped out of the tanks.

I'm starting to feel out of my depth.

Handy hint

Don't touch the seacocks unless the captain tells you to. You might sink the boat!

Fresh air can be let in through two snorkel tubes on the top of the submarine, but they have to be lowered before the boat dives. The crew must remember to close the air valves, or water will rush in.

17

Disaster!

t's 29 August 1863, and the *Hunley* is putting to sea for its first mission. Lieutenant John Payne is in command. The crew – all volunteers – are in their seats and the hatches are open. Lieutenant Payne gives the order to get under way, and the crew start turning the propeller. As the *Hunley* moves away from the wharf, Payne climbs down through the forward (front) hatch. Straight away, things go wrong. Within seconds, the *Hunley* is heading for the seabed!

What happened?

1. TANGLED. As Payne climbs down into the submarine, he gets tangled in one of the mooring lines that tie it to the wharf.

4. CHARLES HASKER fights his way out of the forward hatch against the torrent of water pouring in, but the hatch cover slams down on his leg.

3. LIEUTENANT PAYNE escapes from the forward hatch. Two sailors scramble out through the aft hatch.

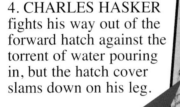

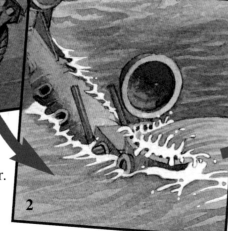

2. STRUGGLING to get free, he steps on the dive-plane lever. The submarine's nose dips under the surface and water pours through the open hatch.

5. THE FORCE of water pressing down on the hatch cover makes it impossible to lift. Hasker is dragged all the way down to the seabed.

6. ESCAPE. The *Hunley* fills up
with water. Now the water pressure
is the same inside and out. This
makes the hatch cover
easier to lift, and at last
Hasker is able to get his
leg free.

6

7. FREE AT LAST!
Hasker is the last person
to escape from the
submarine. The rest of
the crew are drowned.

7

Disaster strikes again

The *Hunley* is raised from the seabed by salvage ships and put back into service. A new volunteer crew is led by Horace Hunley himself – the man the submarine is named after.

On 15 October 1863 the *Hunley* is practising how to attack an enemy ship. It heads towards its pretend target – really a friendly ship, the *Indian Chief* – and dives below it. When it surfaces on the other side, a dummy torpedo towed behind the submarine bumps up against the ship's hull. If this were a real attack, the torpedo would explode. At 9.25am the *Hunley* sets off for another practice run.

> We'll show them what modern technology can do!

CAPTAIN HUNLEY checks the direction with his compass – once the sub is submerged, he won't be able to see where the target is.

BATTEN DOWN THE HATCHES! The fore and aft hatches are closed and sealed shut. Then the submarine dives below the waves.

SAILORS on the *Indian Chief* watch the submarine dive, then rush to the other side of the ship to see it come up again.

Any minute now, boys...

THE SAILORS spot bubbles on the surface, but the submarine does not appear. It has sunk with all its crew. This time there are no survivors.

Oh my! That doesn't look good.

DIVERS go down and search for the missing submarine. They soon find it lying on the seabed with its nose jammed into the sticky mud.

RAISED AGAIN. The divers pass cables under the *Hunley* and salvage ships pull it up to the surface. Its forward water valve, or seacock, is found open. That's why it sank.

Amazingly, even after these two disasters, people still volunteer to serve on the *Hunley*, and a third crew is soon found.

Final mission

The *Hunley* now tries a new way of attacking, without having to dive under the enemy ship. An iron spar, or pole, about 5 metres long is fitted to its nose. An explosive torpedo is attached to the pole. The torpedo has a sharp spear point to make it stick into a wooden ship's hull. The plan is to ram the torpedo into the ship's hull and then back away to a safe distance before exploding it. On 17 February 1864 the *Hunley* goes into action against a Union warship, USS *Housatonic*.

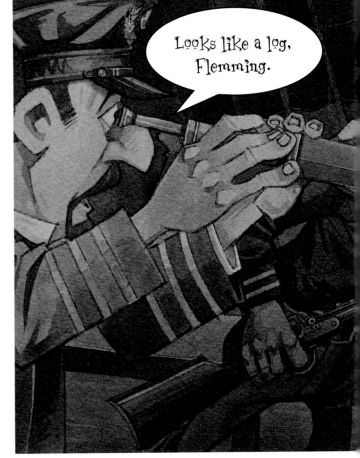

Looks like a log, Flemming.

Battle stations!

INSIDE THE DARK and cramped *Hunley*, the crew crank the propeller as fast as they possibly can to pick up speed.

THE *HUNLEY'S* PROPELLER turns so fast that it churns up the water and leaves a trail of foaming white waves behind it.

ALARM! As soon as the *Hunley* is spotted, a gong is banged on the *Housatonic* to bring the crew rushing to battle stations.

ON TARGET. The long spar on the *Hunley*'s bow rams into the *Housatonic*'s wooden hull and sticks fast.

Handy hint

Don't get seasick. There's nowhere to lie down.

That's no log, sir!

On board the Housatonic, *lookout Robert Flemming is the first to spot the strange object in the water.*

BOOM!

THE CREW start cranking the propeller in the opposite direction. The submarine backs away from the *Housatonic*, leaving the torpedo stuck firmly in its hull. Then the captain pulls a rope to explode the torpedo.

THE EXPLOSION rips a hole in the *Housatonic*'s hull and it sinks quickly, stern first. The water is shallow and most of the *Housatonic*'s crew survive by climbing into the rigging.

SOLDIERS on shore see a light in the water. Is it the *Hunley*, signalling that the mission was a success? They light a fire to guide it home, but the *Hunley* never returns.

Finding the Hunley

The *Hunley*'s third crew do not survive their mission, but they have made history: it's the first time ever that a submarine has attacked and sunk an enemy warship.

In the 1980s, scientists start a search for the *Hunley*. They search around the wreck of the *Housatonic*, but find nothing. But in 1995, divers go back and look again. In just over 8 metres of water, about 300 metres from the *Housatonic*, a diver pushes a pole down into the seabed. A metre down, the pole hits something hard. The diver clears some sediment and feels a curved shape. At first he thinks it's a pipe, but then he feels a hinge. It's a hatch cover! He has found the *Hunley*!

Who owns the Hunley?

It's ours.

It's ours.

It's definitely ours.

WHEN THE *HUNLEY* is found, someone must decide who it belongs to. The state of South Carolina claims it because the wreck lies off its coast.

THE STATE OF ALABAMA also puts in a claim for the *Hunley*, because it was built there. But in the end, neither South Carolina nor Alabama wins its claim.

THE US GOVERNMENT points out that all Confederate property became US government property after the war. The other parties finally agree.

25

Raise the Hunley!

The *Hunley* is to be raised, but after more than 130 years on the seabed no-one knows how strong it is. If it's lifted in the wrong way, it might fall apart. A strong steel frame is specially built for the job. A floating crane lowers it carefully until it sits above the *Hunley*. Divers pass 32 straps under the *Hunley* and attach the ends of these to the frame. Finally, on 8 August 2000, the floating crane hoists the whole thing to the surface.

THE *HUNLEY* IS OPENED by taking off a panel on the top. Inside, the whole submarine is full of fine black sediment.

Steady as she goes!

SCIENTISTS CAREFULLY scrape the sediment away. It smells like rotten eggs! After a few days, they start finding objects belonging to the *Hunley*'s last crew.

Even now that the Hunley *has been raised and studied, scientists still don't know why it sank for the third time.*

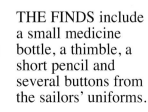

THE FINDS include a small medicine bottle, a thimble, a short pencil and several buttons from the sailors' uniforms.

THE REMAINS of the crewmen are found too. They are buried with full military honours in Charleston, South Carolina, near the graves of other former crewmen of the *Hunley*.

After the Hunley

**A**s you riveted the *Hunley*'s iron plates together, back in 1863, you couldn't help wondering whether submarines had any future. The sub that you built couldn't go very fast and couldn't dive very deep – and it killed most of the people who served on it.

If you could magically come back 140 years later, you'd be amazed by how much submarines have changed. A US *Ohio*-class submarine is a giant vessel, heavier than 2,200 *Hunleys*, and it can dive 40 times deeper.

MODERN SUBMARINES avoid hitting things by using sound. The crew can hear sounds made by nearby vessels. They also send out sound signals and listen for echoes bouncing back from nearby objects. This is called *sonar*.

THERE'S NO SIGN of sailors turning a propeller by hand! Today, the most advanced submarines have nuclear engines. The nuclear fuel heats water to make steam. The steam turns a turbine – like wind turning a windmill's sails, but much faster. The spinning turbine drives a generator that makes electricity. The electricity powers a motor, which turns the propeller.

MODERN SUBMARINES don't have to ram a ship to attack it. They fire self-propelled torpedoes that can track their targets.

THE BIGGEST SUBMARINES are armed with rocket-powered missiles that can travel thousands of kilometres.

Glossary

Aft A sailor's word for 'rear'.

Ballast Any kind of weight that is added to a boat to make it more stable, or to a submarine to make it sink.

Blockade To close off an enemy area so that people or supplies cannot move in or out.

Bow The front end of a boat.

Cable A strong rope.

Cutwater A kind of fin fitted to a part of a boat to streamline it, so it slips through the water more easily.

Deadlight A small, thick glass window that does not open.

Depth gauge An instrument for measuring how far beneath the water a submarine is.

Dive plane A fin that can be tilted down or up to make the submarine dive or surface.

Forward (pronounced 'forrad') A sailor's word for 'front'.

Hatch A narrow doorway on a boat. The door itself is called a **hatch cover**.

Nuclear engine An engine that uses the power created by splitting atoms.

Periscope A device using mirrors that allows you to see things that are higher up than you are. Modern submarines have periscopes so that the crew can see what is above the surface.

Port A small round window.

Rigging The ropes on a sailing ship that support and control the sails.

Rudder A hinged flap at the back of a boat, used for steering.

Salvage To recover a boat or cargo that has been lost at sea.

Seacock A valve that lets seawater into a boat.

Sediment Soft mud that has settled at the bottom of a sea or lake.

Snorkel tube A breathing tube of the kind used by divers in shallow water.

Sonar An electronic device that detects objects underwater by sending out sound pulses and listening for the echoes that come back.

Spar A sailor's word for 'pole'.

Stern The back end of a boat.

Tiller The lever that turns the rudder.

Torpedo An underwater bomb. Modern torpedoes have engines, but early ones did not, and had to be towed or pushed.

Turbine A windmill-like machine that can drive an electricity generator.

Valve A device like a tap, that can be opened to let water flow or closed to stop it flowing.

Volunteer A person who agrees to do something without being forced to do it. All the sailors on the *Hunley* were volunteers – they served on the submarine because they wanted to.

Wharf A place by the waterside where boats can be tied up for loading or unloading.

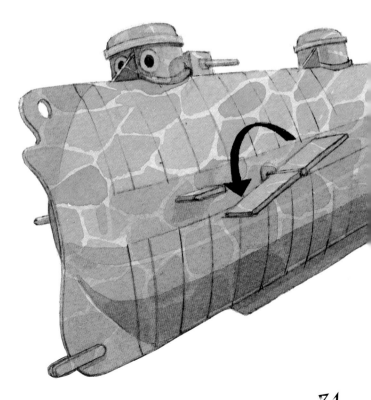

Index